WOMAN POWER:

Top 10 Tips To Excel As A Womanpreneur

TABLE OF CONTENTS

Introduction…………………………..3

Chapter One

1.1: Understanding the concept of entrepreneurship………………………..4

1.2: Women Entrepreneurship………….5

Chapter Two

2.1: Getting started……………………..6

Chapter Three

3.1: Drivers of Success as a Womanpreneur……………………….20

Conclusion…………………………….27

Introduction

Nowadays, ladies have advanced to accomplish great feats in different areas. The truth of the matter is they are moving side by side with men giving them a test. You might be anxious to turn into a successful Womanpreneur like the others. Provided that this is true, then you would want to figure out how to start a business right without any preparation and make a domain from it. Going through a few master tips can assist with accomplishing your fantasy.

Patience Matthew is an economist and business expert managing her own fashion business. Her passion for exploits in entrepreneurship has birthed this book.

CHAPTER ONE

1.1: Understanding the concept of Entrepreneurship

Business alludes to the idea of creating and dealing with an undertaking to acquire benefits by facing a few challenges in the corporate world. The most common way of setting up a business is known as ***business venturing*** or ***entrepreneurship***.

Entrepreneurship is the creation or extraction of monetary worth. Thus, it can be seen as change, for the most part, embracing risk is what is ordinarily experienced in beginning a business, which might incorporate different qualities than just monetary ones.

An entrepreneur is a person who makes and oversees a business venture, bearing a large portion of the dangers and getting a charge out of the greater part of the prizes known as ***profits***.

1.2: Women Entrepreneurship

A lady business visionary can likewise be known as a ***womanpreneur***. A womanpreneur is a person who applies lady-like qualities and approaches through business ventures, fully intent on working on the personal satisfaction and prosperity of other you g ladies. Many are doing as much by establishing "*for ladies, by ladies*" endeavors. Womanpreneurs are propelled to enter business markets by the craving to make abundance and social change, in view of the morals of collaboration, balance and shared regard. These undertakings can have the impact of both strengthening and liberation.

CHAPTER TWO

2.1: Getting started

To assist ladies in business with beginning on their endeavors, from associating with other female business visionaries to gaining admittance to capital. Here are tips for ladies business visionaries to go into business:

1. Remember It Takes Time

While building your woman-owned business, remember that it takes time to start making a profit. Don't drop everything. Instead, keep your day job and build your business after hours.

First try to determine the reason to start a business and not just do a job. This particular criterion will help you understand whether you will fail or succeed in your new venture. You need to have passion and a firm reason to start a business. This very reason will help guide you to your mission. Remember, you will have to face the ups & downs in business while moving towards your goals. Don't expect everything to happen overnight.

Be prepared to invest time and effort into your business, but don't forget to enjoy the ride as well!

2. Connect With Other Female Entrepreneurs

There are a lot of like-minded women who are starting businesses, and there are a lot of women-focused groups. Some are based locally, in an industry, or even nationwide. Participate in these groups to build a network with other female entrepreneurs. No one understands your predicament better than another female entrepreneur, whether it's introducing a new client, an investor, or someone to vent to about the problems of running a business. Some key tips for building a resourceful team include:

- Creating strong relationships with people you trust.
- Being willing to ask for help and delegating tasks when possible. By building a team that is supportive and helpful, female entrepreneurs can achieve their goals.

3. Have Confidence in Yourself and Your Business

Getting into a business as a lady, the main weapon in your stockpile ought to be your certainty. You're nearly there on the off chance that you accept that you can make it happen. Business venture follows no inflexible construction and seems to be a flight of stairs. It's essential to keep your confidence and realize that the troublesome way forward is beneficial which necessitates your commitment. As ladies, we can assist with sustaining a creative business scene that is different, open minded, and hopes to help the world.

Self-conviction is particularly pivotal to making progress in any business. On the other hand, ladies are found to underestimate their capacities. On the off chance that you don't have confidence in yourself, then you can not anticipate that others should trust in your administrations or items. In the event that you feel less sure about your capacities, no investor would be intrigued to make invest in your business. Additionally your staffs are probably not going to give 100 percent of their best productive output. This is on the grounds that ailing in fearlessness, you can't rouse them to do better. Many female business people accept that they must be wonderful before they can begin their business. They additionally accept that their womanliness will keep them away from prevailing in business.

4. Be the Face of Your Company

As an entrepreneur, you are probably going to have your web-based entertainment profiles saw oftentimes. You can utilize serious areas of strength for a brand to build the perceivability of your private venture. This will permit others to consider you to be an insightful, vital pioneer and depend on your organization much more.

5. Don't Let Impostor Syndrome Hold You Back

One obstruction a few ladies face while beginning a business is *'an inability to embrace success'* otherwise known as **"impostor syndrome"** which can incapacitate. Female business people frequently put an excessive amount of accentuation on others' assessments of their business thoughts. They neglect to have faith in themselves and their own thoughts. Re-thinking choices and feeling brimming with tension can negatively affect their business thought's advancement. Recall that nobody, not even yourself, ought to disrupt the general flow when you accept what you are doing is advantageous.

Business not entirely settled by the reasoning example of the business visionary at the hour of its starting. The right disposition and approach can assist you with making sure progress in your endeavor. You shouldn't believe yourself to be the more vulnerable orientation. Attempt to oversee and beat issues as best as could really be expected. Just you are a woman doesn't mean you will make sure and speedy progress. Maybe you want to leave your usual range of familiarity. Rather than stressing over others' thought process, center around what you accept and a big motivator for you. Be enthusiastic about your business and ensure each and every individual who you work with shares in that enthusiasm. At the point when individuals are motivated by the thing you're doing, they are bound to help you.

6. Get Access to Capital

This initial step is certainly not a severe prerequisite yet is most certainly suggested. One significant stage in beginning your private venture is knowing how to get to capital. This can be difficult for ladies entrepreneurs simply beginning. In the first place, ensure you have a relationship with your financial institution. This will be key while applying for loans, similar to an individual credit extension or a private company advance.

Second, make major areas of strength for an arrangement. You will require this when the opportunity arrives to acquire cash. There are many difficulties to beginning a business, yet not approaching capital ought not be one of them.

7. Acquire essential business skills

Not all business people are conceived perfect. Maybe some foster through hard times work and assurance. In the event that, you don't have a place with a business family, then, at that point, you are to foster yours. A purposeful lady business visionary is one who can foster fundamental pioneering abilities during recreation hours. Instead of messing about or shopping, you might peruse a book on business or go to a workshop.

Ladies in these organizations have been set in comparable circumstances and confronted comparable battles as other youngster ladies business visionaries.

8. Start Before You're Ready

Perfectionists beware! Starting a small business is tough. There will always be a part of it that you are unprepared for. There will always be a reason to wait. Don't do that. Start before you're ready. You'll learn along the way and when you need help, ask. People want to help you when you are doing something difficult, like starting a business!

9. Build a Strong Team

One of my most significant hints is to encircle yourself with a solid group. As ladies in a generally male-ruled field, we can at times want to or believe we can do everything ourselves. Notwithstanding, appointment and help for errands is similarly pretty much as significant as your own time speculation. While beginning, recognize the three most significant features of your business, and recruit representatives or employees in like manner. In particular, I suggest zeroing in your enrollment endeavors on:

- Computerized showcasing
- Funds and planning
- Creation of executives

This will guarantee that you have opportunity and energy to zero in on advancement and needle-moving development.

10. Be Tenacious

As a lady in business, it can frequently be hard to break into a few specific enterprises. Nonetheless, as any lady knows, being relentless is part of our DNA. We can outfit that resource for guarantee that we don't take 'no' for a response and that we'll return to the drawing board as the need might arise to.

This drive impels us towards progress as well as it sets a phenomenal model until the end of the group, where you'll see inventiveness and efficiency flourish. Indeed, even the best women entrepreneurs have had times when they wanted to abandon their venture, however they endured, thanks to their commitment and assurance. Keep in mind, achievement is rarely ensured, however with hardwork and determination, the sky is but a stepping stones.

CHAPTER THREE

3.1: Drivers of Success as a Womanpreneur

Initiative orientation uniqueness simply termed *'Leadership Gender Disparity'* remains obstinately high. Studies have shown that one justification for this is the oblivious predisposition that leads individuals to respond distinctively to male and female pioneers. For example, male desire is frequently commended while conversely, female aspiration frequently brings about antagonism. Additionally, ladies are supposed to be more merciful, moral and greater at fashioning splits than men.

An effective pioneer moves, propels, coaches and coordinates others toward a more significant standard. We should be straightforward accomplishing more in the event that you are a lady in our male-overwhelmed business world is somewhat difficult. Productive women entrepreneurs have normal characteristics found in all great chiefs, for example, being emphatic, move disapproved, risk-making, critical, still up in the air as well as have a refusal to surrender in taking your business to a higher level. Here are a few characteristics any fruitful Womanpreneur ought to have;

1. Integrity

This alludes to the demonstration of sticking to moral or moral standards and keeping your promise. It is essential to compelling leadership. People need to follow a leader who acts with honesty, since they would be rest assured they'll be dealt with reasonably and that their leader will give a valiant effort for the association. Likewise, it spurs trust with individuals, from the representatives you lead, to the investors and accomplices you bring, to the clients you serve. Moreover, moral way of behaving, genuineness and regard beginning at the top are pivotal to making an organization develop in view of those qualities.

2. Humility and a willingness to learn

Entrepreneurship (i.e Business venture) is a long lasting cycle, and clever businessmen figure that out. The business world changes so quick that you can be a developed today and be out of date tomorrow. Productive women entrepreneurs continue to learn and concentrate on their goal that they can adjust to the steadily changing pattern quickly. They humble themselves and realize whenever the open door emerges.

3. Resilience and persistence

Regardless of your orientation, business is testing and brimming with vulnerability. With the heavier responsibilities ladies carry on and the log jam in professional force that frequently accompanies having children the test is made considerably more perplexing. However, a great many ladies fabricate organizations because of their flexibility and diligence. In business, no good thing comes simple. To succeed, you should try sincerely and persevere in what you need. Diligence is important to develop as a financial specialist.

4. Intuition

Ladies have areas of strength for an instinct. As well as utilizing realities and information to direct their choices, solid female pioneers can likewise take advantage of their instinct for direction. Instinct is much of the time what guides them through the highs and lows of business. Ladies are likewise proficient at perusing their groups and spotting potential pain points. Utilizing this expertise, they can construct steadfast groups of representatives who feel esteemed and understood.

5. Adaptability

Making a move is fundamental, yet a profound comprehension ought to illuminate it regarding your clients, your industry and your market. Women are interested and open to novel thoughts. Flexibility well empowers us to see changes coming for the business, which is particularly significant in this time of rapid change driven by innovation.

6. Communication skills

Correspondence and authority remain closely connected. Ladies are not just great at talking, they're additionally commonly great at tuning in and hearing too. Correspondence goes past talking. Ladies have an inborn capacity to see non-verbal communication and sentiments. Having a profound comprehension of what drives individuals, ladies are superb inspirations for their groups.

7. Empathy

Ladies are socially molded to be more compassionate. We normally act as guardians and peacekeepers. The impending ages esteem investing energy with their families and their psychological well-being more than their ancestors, and they search for managers who grasp their remarkable conditions. Employers can make steadfast workers by relating with them on a *close-to-home level*.

8. Strong support system

It is normal for effective ladies to help their female partners, champion ladies in the working environment and help other people rise the company pecking order. Ladies are more averse to be "solitary individuals" or "heads of the pack," loaning themselves normally to helping other people. As ladies, we should uphold one another and take a stab at acknowledgment and backing in our nearby networks, on the web and in our businesses, by impacting navigation and foundational change.

CONCLUSION

Ladies are establishing businesses and organizations at a phenomenal rate, and for good explanation: with such countless open doors accessible to us, there is no reason not to hold onto them! From defining limits and making an unmistakable vision for your business to systems administration and excelling at marketing, these tips will assist you with taking your business to a higher level.